ファ C0/BPD-880

LA COMMEDIA SOTTERRANEA

della

Macchina da Scrivere

ADVANCE
READER
COPY
PUBLICATION DATE:
MAR 1 2019

PELEKINESIS

NEW YORK † LONDON † SYDNEY † LOS ANGELES

La Commedia Sotterranea della Macchina da Scrivere:
A First Folio from the Typewriter Underground
(Collection of Swizzle Felt)

ISBN: 978-1-949790-08-5

eISBN: 978-1-949790-09-2

(TwU text: © Marc Zegans/TwU images: © Eric Edelman.)

Text: Marc Zegans
Artwork: Eric Edelman
Layout and book design by Mark Givens

First Pelekinesis Printing 2019

For information:
Pelekinesis, 112 Harvard Ave #65, Claremont, CA 91711 USA

PUBLISHING GROUP
www.pelekinesis.com

LA COMMEDIA SOTTERRANEA
della Macchina da Scrivere

A First Folio from the Typewriter Underground
(Collection of Swizzle Felt)

FORWARD

My life and position as host of what some have called the Salon Du Claque, a gathering of typists that has attained an immodest degree of notoriety, has brought me into contact with fellow members and early documenters of an affiliation of affinity for the ribbon, key, platen and spool—the Typewriter Underground. The subterranean world of type, by turns romantic and revanchist, doubtful and dissident, horny and heterodox, was not custodial by nature. Long before the Penumbra, well in advance of the Carbonites, and preceding by far the entry of commercial interests intent on reproduction for profit, collecting, archiving and retention were rarely considered. The Underground lived for the struck key, the pulled sheet and the thrill of receiving a smudged original passed by hand, source often unknown.

With time the early sheets became tattered, torn, tongued and lost. Few originals remained, their existence frequently known only by those who possessed them. Documentation of the Underground was little different. Underground journalists and historians hewed to the code of the single text—"Type it once; copy never!" Though pirated copies were sometimes made, and, later, commissioned reproductions acquired through the good offices of the Transcriptionistas, original documentation was frequently mislaid, soaked or otherwise destroyed as it traveled from hand to hand, or was yanked from reading posts and thereby lost to posterity. Complete and original historical accounts of the emergent and early Underground are now rare, and sheets from the primal typists less common than Gutenbergs. More often than not collectors and archivists must content themselves with conserved fragments, low-grade third and fourth generation copies of dubious accuracy, oddities and discards snatched from the wastebaskets of principal typers.

Though I fancy and often indulge the peculiar pleasure of burning fresh sheets, and while I relish the public reading and shredding of original type, rendering the rare accessible to a chosen few gives me a Nabokovian frisson of delight. The simple thought of sharing the contents of the rarest of sheets in limited quantity sends a shiver along my spine and most delightfully lifts the hairs on the back my neck. With such sensual delight as my companion, through the good offices of my personal librarian, Edamame Phelps, and my wine steward and sage advisor, Horace Nepenthe Jones, I have assembled through purchase, barter, theft and extortion a remarkable collection of sheets documenting in type and provocative collage the origins, social customs and characters that gave life to the Underground.

Culled from this larger and most private collection, you will find here a folio of seminal prints and hitherto unseen verse fragments that in their variety, perspicuity, strangeness and delight call to life the Underground I have known, fostered, indulged and underwritten. In keeping with tradition, the sheets, enfolded and boxed remain unbound, so that you may enjoy the distinct pleasure of taking up a single leaf, and then another, as the night grows long, the brandy warm and the imagination ever more wild. May your spine shiver with delight.

~ As always,
Swizzle Felt

DESIGN OF THE COMMEDIA

Following on the inspired example of King's Men Heminge and
Condell, who gathered for publication the works of Bacon, de Vere,
Marlowe and Stanley, and those of Earls Oxford and Derby, drawing
into unity the oft-played scripts of bards anonymous, and conveying
them to the care and ministration of Messrs. Blount and Jaggard—
who shrewdly these presented under Avonian and Stratfordonian
stamp, rendering with a shake of salt this collection of plays and
wrights into a Leviathan of stage (crossing vex'd Bermooths) without
peer—we have congregated, curated and compiled a commedia
of typewritten poetries, histories, and bluff biographies hitherto
un-joined, and in their assembly revealed the mountainous inver-
sion on such stuff as the *Typewriter Underground* is made on.

In crafting this *folio*, the first such endeavor of its patron and
peerless patroon, Swizzle Felt, we approached the limited repro-
duction of unique sheets documenting the Underground and its
originating players with unchaste reverence for the sanctity of the
Underground's cardinal form—the single key-struck page— deter-
mining to leave the contents unbound, even as we replicated with
exquisite fidelity that not meant to be duped. This preservation of
source and violation of intent expresses utterly the libertine connois-

seurship that gives swizzle to Felt's myriad endeavors, and that allows us to share with you this jauntily constructed collection of works that define, delineate, characterize and exemplify the Underground and its dappled denizens.

One enters the *folio,* produced in an edition of one hundred, excluding artist's proofs, through the door of a dancehall, encountering a trance inducing *Milonga,* expressive of the longing for the lost ephemerality, physicality, and analogue eccentricity of the last pre-digital age. One exits on the howl of a blue-flowered coyote undertaking a cyclic annunciation of forgiveness. Between these sheets are histories, reveries, character sketches and collages formed in and from fragments of verse, authors unknown, forming between these a commedia della vita that will animate for you, our dear reader, that which has been, and yet may be, the *Typewriter Underground*

Edamame Phelps
Librarian Particulier to Swizzle Felt

TABLE OF FRAGMENTS

Dear reader, please note that this table contains both numbered and unnumbered fragments. Numbering in the table corresponds to the relevant fragment's assigned location in the classified partition of the larger Felt Collection. Not all fragments presented here were plucked from the pigeonholed portion. Accordingly, these lack numbers. In addition, the ordering of numbered fragments herein does not hew to the sequence in the Felt Collection. If you are confused, we are delighted, and vice versa.

~ SF, EP & HNJ

* * *

Fragment XVI: Alpha Betsy

Fragment XVII: Limpet Residue

Fragment XIX: Manicotti II

Fragment XX: (The most famous of the early writings. Known to all as "Prolixity.")

Quarantine Ellipsis

Incomplete Sentences – Includes "For Your Dégustation."

The Bone Fragments

Fragment XXII: The Hunt and Pecks

Doings at the Cheesy Cover (parts i and ii)

Samizdat

CODA

Hyacinth Coyote

TABLE OF ILLUSTRATIONS

PRELUDE

Milonga

Cultivating memories of a life but imagined,
more than passion, a desire beyond duende,
a yearning for longing, conjured by dance a saudade
for a past that would have been worth the longing

The sound of piano, squeezebox, and typewriter
playing in a dusty, tired-floored stucco dancehall
in a melancholy black-and-white fever-dream
in a mood for lost love never had, nor was

The dancers. backward traveling to Angel Villoldo,
heels conjuring the clacque of the Salon de Tango
eye-locking lean frames in perpetual Orillero
travelling past the ghost orchestra of Pichuco

Their exhaustion keeps them from wondering,
"What will happen when, with the sun, this milonga ends?"
the warmth of their damp-through-cloth long bodies gone to chill
in the dawn graveyard of the workday life

Their exhaustion dissolves all but the floor, the lights, the walk
the turn, the tilt, the entwining of legs, the release,
the burgundy-print wrap-dress-ladies in chairs waiting,
hoping for a dance before they dissolve with the dawn,

never knowing if they have entered the typist's heart
which summons them nightly from the land of their sad dreams
to the dim incandescence of this hall of violins,
a soft habanera rising from the page.

EXPOSITION

I

The Typewriter Underground

It started, they say, with a clack in a tunnel
that gathered the restless, the impatient
the disconnecting and the disconnected.

A circle formed in soot and ash, amidst
the broken rock, beneath the track-bed
Olivettis and Underwoods at the stations

of the clock, typists looking inward.
And from the circle emerged smudged piles
of foolscap and onion skin, corrasable

bond, linen, cotton laid and handpaper
pourous and rough, unspooling through rollers
carriages returning with a smack.

One day, Curious and Curiouser
twins formerly known as the two Carols
arrived with triangular partners' desk

salvaged from the defunct ladvertising
firm, Morbidly, Sincere, Della Femina
placing it firmly at circle's center

seating themselves before their instruments
leaving the third side with the typewriter ghost
and a looped recording blaring, "is Holy"

through a cracked cassette-deck three inch speaker
that entrained the oracular typists
whose utterances lifted through subway grates

like steam to the street, evaporating
before they could be seized, codified, linked
tagged, tweeted, liked, loved, laughed at, and shared.

but all that came later.

III

The screeds, pamphlets, papers, books and broadsides
followed by fictions, fantasies and verse
emerged as exquisite corpses

from the serial constructions typer-
on-typer splayed across the turning page
until Steppins' *House of a Thousand Ribalds*

forever changed the Underground.
It was Steppins, always Steppins
and his tales of Victorian lust

that catalyzed the contention
that made the Typewriter Underground
into something more than an hobby.

II

Clytaemnestra Litotes the catalyst
perhaps, or perhaps the detonator
before she exited to sell soft-serve

at a roadside stand eight miles from Albany
occupied a shimmering central place
in the founding myth, but was she real? — no one knew.

and yet the typewriters clacked with her tales
or tales of her, or who she became
until she was simply typewriter trope

a nodding symbol of recognition
among denizens of, pretenders to
and clackers in The Typewriter Underground.

IV

Fructose Lysander,
the son of a food industry chemist
and a failed Shakespearean actor
was the first diagnosed case of "the clacks"
a discontinuous tinnitus
appearing to the ear as a typhoon
of typewriter key-strikes.

Lysander's case of "the clacks"
as it came to be called
baffled audiologists
otolaryngologists
neurologists and country quacks,

until a French neurosurgeon
most fond of diagnostic
speculation, declared
Lysander's condition to be
the product of "neural absence,"
a condition under which

the young Fructose's ear
reconstructed without sequence
order or pattern, the missing
mechanical sounds (dimly
recalled via genetic memory)
of the pre-digital past.

It arrived, he asserted
in "un éclat mechanique"
as the brain desperately sought
to bring pattern to memory
outside direct experience.

As curative prescription
Lysander was provided

An ancient brass-keyed, pur sang
enamel typewriter, employed
said some, by the proprietor
of Paris's finest, and most
discrete opium den

whose slim, privately published
narcotic novels, entitled,
"Les Affaires Un, Deux, Trois, Quartre, &tc.
were know to have magnetized
the attention of Burroughs
when he discovered them packed
in a trim leather valise

mistakenly grouped with his luggage
on his famous trip to Tangier
and achieved thrift store influence
as rock stars with pretensions to poetry
les contre-intellectuals
and les nouvelle-vague écrivains
known as les auteurs manqué

or the mistaken writers
sought out the few copies
remaining in used bookstores
and antiquarian shops.
His prescription with the red
enamel typewriter
roughly translated, was to type

until you have dominated
entirely the clack, and brought
order and full expression
to the mechanical
imperative now filling
your auditory complex
with the chaos of echo

absent primary signal
the defines the condition
of your clattering neural lack.
(The neurosurgeon took pride
in using more words than needed
imagining that the excess
elevated pronouncements

above the plebian discourse
of diagnosis and cure
to the plane of grand theory—
he ached to be remembered
as a philosophe neurosurgical!)
And so began the typing
that led Lysander from his

auditory hell, into
the production of vital
musical compositions
resulting with astonishing
speed, in a collection
of orchestral scores, known as
les symphonies typographique.

Conductors urgently struggled
to master his constantly
evolving notations.
Principal violinists
were overcome with compulsions
to develop technique mécanique
appropriate to what they termed

Fructosian compositional
mediations, and as word
of his devices spread into
popular awareness
scores of previously closeted
individuals beset with "the clacks"
came forward to share their woes.

Some, of course, were fakers
type-key junkies frequenting
key mills, when the regular
channels were denied them
but others, like Lysander
surfacing in the demi-monde
soon formed circles of typing

in which they found bonhomie
and perhaps some small relief
from their clackish isolation—
and the Typewriter Underground
was growing, emerging from
isolated practice into
sub-vocal cultural pulse.

VI

The Theater Of Delay

Bayreuth Schtreb ToCoccus had the rare knack
For conceptualizing art moments.

After the triumph of his Ballet Juste
The most lavishly funded company
In the history of dance, a brilliant
Fusion of hubris and social justice
Premised on the claim that training, talent

Choreography, lights and audience
Irrevocably prejudiced the dance—
"Why," he asked, "should dance in society
privilege dancers and audiences
whose convergence is based on selection,

When selection of any form excludes?
Does not choosing on the basis of skill
Exclude? Does not choosing on strength exclude?
Does not choosing by lottery exclude?
Does not choosing on ticket price exclude?

Does not choosing prevent the Ballet Juste?
The true Ballet Juste," he boldly announced,
"must be the ballet of all daily life, performed
all the time without distinction between
venue and street, ticket and seat.

In such a ballet documentation
Would be irrelevant because the dance
Shifting always would not permit review.
Without need for accountability
Money could be spent without risk or guilt.

There would be no one to alienate
Because the production would include all

And seek to change the behavior of none
The Ballet Juste's success would be achieved
The moment its funders claimed all credit."

Foundations were ecstatic, "ToCoccus,"
They said, "you are genius in purest form,
We celebrate your bold innovation
And offer you awards and many grants."
"Too kind," he said, while pocketing the checks.

He needed to succeed himself quickly,
And began scouring the demimonde
for a subcultural pulse he could use,
and it could not be in the field of dance—
ToCoccus had learned never to repeat.

"A pairing of typewriter and theater
or perhaps, better put, 'An immersion.'
No, 'A potentiation of the clacque!'
I will deconstruct improvisation!"

"Theater," he proclaimed, "is a total lie!
It is not a suspension, but a lie!
A lie against neurological truth!
For theater purports to be in real time
And yet perception follows stimulus

They do not overlap for an instant!
We do not perceive this miniscule gap,
But it is there destroying truth on stage!
There is only one means to make theater true,
We must honestly demonstrate the gap,

Bringing it directly onto the stage!
To introduce truth into staged drama,
We must create a `Theatre of Delay!'
I will commission its first production
A groundbreaking work entitled, `The Pause.'

`The Pause' will follow the nominal tropes
of a night with an improv theater troupe
with one fundamental, cleansing difference—
on the stage, paired one-to-one with actors
will be typists of the highest order.

It will be the typist who responds first
To prompts thrown out by audience members,
or to the preceding line voiced on stage
it will be the typist, not the actor
who creates, in situ, a script fragment

delivered rapidly by copy-boy
to the thespian awaiting her line,
then, the delay having been established,
the separation of brain and voice clear,
the line or action will be presented!

Thus will theater enter the light of truth,
reformulating the dramatic pause
not as amour propre, but amour soi!"
The actors were gathered, the typists found,
And so arrived the "Theater of Delay!"

The Fear of All Sums

Plus signs made Reynard Elocute sweat.
The equals symbol brought tears to his eyes.
The notion that an arbitrary mark
Added to another numeric sign
Made a third that could be separated
Back into these and other possible
Combinations that would yield the same sum
Sent him hurtling under his fine bed.

Sent to a public school on Bassett Road
Kensington at age four, young Elocute
Was asked to glue a picture of a horse
To a thin, rough, rust-covered, staple-bound book
Filled with flimsy, close-spaced, light-blue lined pages
In which he was to copy down his sums.

Arithma gives me the tics he announced
His head, neck and facial muscles jerking
Each time he was compelled to scribe two numbers
A cross, a line beneath, and then a third.
Conjuring the sum was a violent act
A heated cogging of ingot numbers
Pounded into additive billets
The essence of each part lost in the sum.

Elocute feared that participating
In soul stripping merger of the units
Would mint his moral abdication to
Himself being fitted into a mold
Rendering him into uniform likeness
With the other "straight-jacketed clones,"
At four he was told about cloning
More precisely its possibility
On an early winter walk down the street
From the brick house with the bright yellow door
With James Watson of the double helix

Who said that we were the sum of our genes
And that these could be precisely sequenced
Making us, in that sense, replicable.

And so, for Elocute, the copying
Lay in the sum, and summing was danger
For Elocute fiercly wanted to be—
To be Elocute, and uniquely so.
And so Elocute developed the fear
The fear of all sums, and ran to letters.

"There is wiggle-room in analogy"
He would tweedle most happily
Sitting before the tile-lined fireplace
At a small wooden typing desk
Striking the glass keys of his rich maroon
Enameled typewriter, top row covered
Key-by-key-by-key with white tape circles
A reminder that number and symbol

Lurked dangerously beneath the blanks
A horrendous potential destruction
Only a few finger strokes away
And yet unseen and untouched by Reynard
Across the many decades of prosing
As starter yeast for inspired divergence.

DOP

The house of DOP, a bright bouncy castle
Spitting distance from Spuyten Duyvil
With a view past the Chubby Creek
Filled with Harlem Whitefish
Cross Inwood Park, down toward Tubby Hook
Held nary a typewriter, but typists
In ratty coats and coffee stained shirts
Cat glasses and runny black stockings
Streamed over its inflated steps
Plunging into the garish playpen
As if regression into fictive fun
Could recover childhoods never had
For these raised-by-wolves writers in type.

And presiding over the bounce and splash,
The flip and grope of the gravity
Defying, delighted denizens
Of the air-suspended underground,
The magnet of their attraction
In giant-framed, curly-headed splendor,
Self-proclaimed "inflator of the Bounce House,"
Hailing from the land of the lawn guys
Was the long-legged, interview queen, DOP
Who queried typists about their craft
Their preoccupations, their obsessions
And their favorite slices of pizza.

An interview with DOP, it was said,
Rare and cracked as the Portland vase
Was a key to the land beyond type
An opening of the slipstream
Into which idea and medium merged
In rainbow misted torrential flow,
Expressive limitations washed away

In extended waves of orgasm
A departure from form to energy
Immaterial, immaculate
And yet, sticky as an Astro Pop.
An interview with DOP, *it was read.*

35

VIII

The Danger Meditations

Living in the Underground entailed risk.
Typists inhabited the rough margins
of the urban social infrastructure
forming circles in abandoned job shops
transportation tunnels and sub-basements
the roofs of tenements and corner bars
in the lowest rent corners they could find.

And they did not want to draw attention
so they blended with the irreputable
the sketchy, the seamy, the broken, the louche
making themselves targets for shakedowns and more.
The true inhabitants became feral,
Masters and mistresses of feline stealth
Yet, flooding, power-outages, trespass
Theft and casual violence were always near

And much the topic of conversation:
"Did you hear that Lysander's notes were took
And burned as kindling for a warming fire?"
"Three pigeon coops ravaged in the past week."
"Can't wear my transcription drag on the street."
"The dome of our library is showing cracks."

"There's a shortage of black market ribbons
and spools are being hoarded at chop shops."

"Can't carry paper on the street these days
too much risk of being harassed and rolled."
And as the Underground was wont to do
It began to type its experience
First in confessional verse, then in prose
And most famously in meditations.

These meditations and sometime laments
Poured from the scroll of Mechanical Rust
A typist whom many had claimed to have met
But none of whose stories could be proved.
The known details were contradictory
Facts as rare as Robert Johnson photos

Witness accounts of Mechanical's life
Sparkly as a kaleidoscope's glass
Shifting and rearranging constantly
Changing form and gaining embellishment
With each telling. What we cannot dispute
Is the dating of the meditations.
The earliest to appear were Rem-Blick
The middle "Meds" were typed in Lucien

The final verses following the death
By mayhem or suicide of Rust's love
in the elegant type that bore her name
                                    Cassandre Graphika
We have established by typewriter quirks
And characteristics of the paper

The existence of original Rusts
The authentic Danger Meditations.

Examples of Mechanical Rusts Early Danger Meds

i

    I scurry on cobblestone
    Damp sheets pressed
    To my hairless chest

    In-turned shoulders

ii

    Accounting for shadows
    In the Alley at night
    Is fruitless toil.

iii

    I live in the sweat of fear

iv

    We true typists feel danger
    Surrounding us like heavy black cloth.
    The visitors, slumming, feel nothing
                But excitement

      Yet, they are more likely to be rolled.
        What then is danger?

v

    Panting like a wounded canine
    Casandre arrives, lipstick smudged,
        In vigilant terror.

    I pour her Lillet and the story unfolds.

vi

    What do you say to god
    When three typists, young,
    Drown drunk in six inches
    Of grey water from a burst pipe?

    What does god say to you?
    Does the divine speak
         through your fingers?

vii

    What does it mean to lose type?

viii

    Dare danger tell us turn back?
    Dare we listen?

    Which is the true danger?

IX

Seeking sustenance and conversation,
Typers, as they came to be called,
gathered often in the green fluorescence
of Kepler's, "Home of the Elliptical Donut."

They could be found correcting typescript
with Faber-Castell number two pencils
at formica counters in the grubby
morning light, faces pale, beards unshaven

women chewing vintage-store cat glasses
on natural pearl chains made to look plastic,
sipping coffee from chipped and stained white mugs
emblazed with "Kepler's Bottomless Cup."

That was until the great grammatic row,
when a persnickety grammarian
who flew under the flag of Flynn Errol
and fancied himself a red-pencil swashbuckler

less than innocuously enquired,
"Wouldn't it be more correct to say cups?
And, truly, would not mugs be better still?
I will bring this up with Kepler forthwith."

"Snot-filled windbag," one was heard to mutter.
"Copy editor from Hell," said Lindstrom.
"Sharper the pencil, the less they get the point,"
noted Clarabelle Louise Tenefly.

After that Kepler's was never the same,
the steadfast held to their seats, wannabes
looking for entrée arrived in numbers
but the correasable bonhomie

that enlivened the now bleak donut shop
had disappeared like a captured comma
even as the legend of Kepler's spread,
and then came "The Parabolic Croissant."

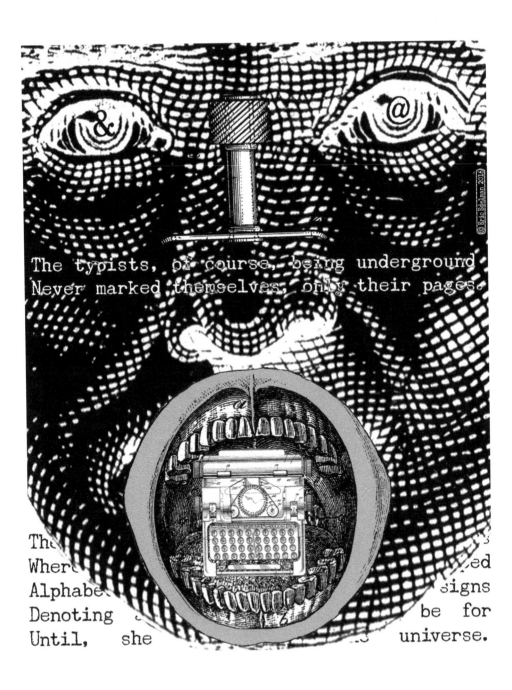

The typists, of course, being underground
Never marked themselves; only their pages.

The
Wher   ed
Alphabe   signs
Denoting   be   for
Until,   she   universe.

© Eric Edelman 2016

XVI

Alpha-Betsy

The Underground Freak-show began with B,
Only if you take her second name first.
Alpha-Betsy Abecedary
Doyenne of the Abecedarium
The temple of underground alpha-bets

Known for her hair, pink as "Lik-m-Aid,"
Strung with letters of many alphabets
And composition of alpha-bet books
That flowed from her like a river of signs
Each title beginning "A is for..."

Until in a bout of synesthesia
She wrote the legendary title, A is four,
And the number-letter book that followed.
French scholars, critics and philosophers
Championed and controverted her work

Reveling in an orgy of lit-crit
Not seen since they abandoned "theory,"
For second homes bought with royalties
And the indulgences of country life
Far from the inconvenience of students.

Alpha-Betsy a self-styled fashion waif,
Who worked by day in a lingerie shop
Selling shoppers sex-toys and camouflage
A path taken after childhood abuse
By religious leaders and family

And early adulthood seducing priests,
As she said, "flipping the script on those fucks,"
Reached enlightenment when an orthodox
Father, traced Cyrillic script on her clit,
Freeing her from her clergy compulsion

And releasing a string of alpha-bets
Through which she reclaimed her childhood
And layer by layer unpeeled her past
For a legion of fans and followers
Who soon created the Great Library

The Alexandria of alpha-bets
Where beneath a high, tiled dome she typed
Alphabet signs upon alphabet signs
Denoting all that letters could be for
Until, she accomplished the universe.

XVII

Limpet Residue

Limpet Residue, né Rodriguez Merch
Afflicted with porphyria since birth
Spent the bulk of his childhood watching
A black and white video loop of
The Incredible Mr. Limpet
In a low-light, windowless cinderblock room
Below the Knickerbocker Apartments
On Thompson Street in Lower Manhattan.

Home schooled and denied all social contact
Until he turned eighteen and was released
Into the world like an injured dolphin
He made his way to the Pyramid Club
Where he soon became a featured artist
Upon crafting the legendary performance piece
Remains of the Limpet, hailed by the press
As, "A witty wander through the residue

of the distorted remains of daytime
Programming by New Jersey's WOR,"
And, "A wise, trenchant and provocative
Deanimation of our inner fish."
He had never heard the word "residue,"
Liked its sound, and attached it to "Limpet"
When reporters began to ask his name.
Now a downtown eminence, he became
Known to art rock legend Tinturn Q. Whine

Who invited Limpet to join forces
In creating the seminal art-band
"signal-to-noise," which Limpet soon reshaped
into the downtown defining, "LintTrap" a
band that entirely removed source
from its auditory output, sending

only distortion, reverb and effects
through their tattered P.A., Mr. Hotdog.

Bored, near death, his skin in tatters, Limpet
Retreated from the music scene, buying
A sticky black Underwood typewriter
From Fritz a ticket-taker novelist
Who worked the Variety Photo-Plays
On Third Avenue, just off Thirteenth Street
Typing bad one page novels between sales
Until his boss told him to knock it off.

Fritz, ever compliant, sold his machine
Limpet took the vintage 1920s
Beauty, bought a sharp thrift-shop fedora
Found himself a typing chamber beneath
a purple-prism, lighted sidewalk door
and began churning out pneumatic prose.

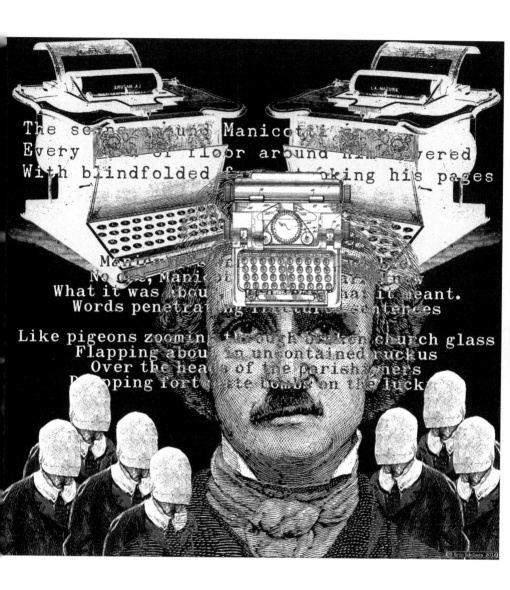

XIX

Manicotti II

Manicotti Delacorte, a Queens born
Builder's son, fashioned a subterranean
Temple of type beneath the weed covered
Octagon ruin on Roosevelt Island.

It is said he spouted type like a fountain
An immense ejaculation of words
Hitting the page in pulsing strophic bursts
Spattering over repeating music

As if he'd gotten a song locked in his head
Riding the Queens Corona bus to school
Which could only be quieted by type
Pounded powerfully on the manual.

His prodigious keystroke speed was legend
His staccato fingers banging the keys
With a jackhammer's speed and subtlety
His periods and exclamation marks

Frequently perforating the white page
His pages developing a texture
So soothing that his followers
Would sit for hours in the anteroom

Eyes closed in scuffed leather club chairs stroking
The paper, as one caresses a cat,
Purring and cooing as their fingers ran
Cross the undulating indentations.

Manicotti's work was unreadable.
No one, Manicotti least of all, knew
What it was about, much less what it meant.
Words penetrating fractured sentences

Like pigeons zooming through broken church glass
Flapping about in uncontained ruckus
Over the heads of the parishioners
Dropping fortunate bombs on the lucky.

The scene around Manicotti grew
Every inch of floor around him covered
With blindfolded fans stroking his pages
And into this scene came a gallerist

Man'l Boone, who proclaimed Manicotti
Progenitor of the "Typewriter Neue"
A method of transmogrification
In which, deprived of sight and meaning

The physical imposition of word on page
Induces a transcendent state of touch
Sensually implicating patron
As partner in erotic frissonage,

And proceeded to install his pages
In a spacious white Chelsea gallery
In a show entitled, "look but don't touch,"
Titillating touch deprived collectors

Permitted to celebrate purchases
In naughtily choreographed blindfold
Touch parties on couches in Boone's "Sense Room."

The year following his epic success
Boone declared Manicotti the magma
Of a transcendent new movement
documented in his new show, *Touch Type*

which Manicotti chose not to attend.

XX

Prolixity Ferris's writing instruments
Were legendary—tile marker for the shower
Wax pencil for glass, henna for her paper skin,
Vintage fountain pens whose nibs cut paper, "just so,"
And an armada of pencils, pens, quills and styli.

Since the day she had formed her first letter, words flowed
And flowed and flowed and flowed, until
She had filled her small world with calligraphy.
If a surface was empty her words flew to it.
And so she became a high master of Yoga.

Through exotic poses arranged into series
That were formally known as "the Pen Asanas,"
She developed almost magic capacity
To cover every inch of her skin with writing
Often flowing from the henna brush in her toes

Onto the small of her back, the back of her thighs
The curve behind her ears, and the lids of her eyes,
Each word in its shape and intent fitted perfect
To its cutaneous locale—a completion
Of a thought suspended until ink it resolved.

What then brought this miraculous hypergraphic
Dakini into the world of typewriter strikes?
Some said it was the adrenaline rush of pure speed.
Others claimed that eyes to page freed her mind
Some said it was the unending brown paper rolls

Which her students and acolytes stole from restrooms
And placed in symmetric columns by her machine
Standing gravely by, like musical page-turners
Ready to seamlessly replace a finished roll
Her typographic flow never interrupted.

The rolls ceremoniously connected end-to-end
By the most fastidious gluists and binders
Became known as the great scroll of Prolixity
And to the mystically inclined, the Wheel of Ferris
Believing that it unwound the cycle of life.

The activity that surrounded Prolixity
Neither attracted nor concerned her. She just typed
And when handed a silk glove by an apostle
Who noticed that she had typed through her right hand skin
She proclaimed, "A glove supreme" and continued on.

52

Quarantine Ellipsis

Quarantine Ellipsis put weight on the pause
"it's the moment between the strokes," she said,
in which everything for the good happens."

Of course, she was also known to remark often,
"I need a rest. I just need a good rest."
She had fashioned a typewriter retreat

in an ancient, family, Millbrook mansion,
a giant room filled with divans, chaise lounges,
fainting couches, day beds, reclining chairs

potions, elixers, relaxants and booze
where she recovered, amidst wind-billowed
sheer curtains blowing in through high windows

from the terrible strains and exhaustions
of her encounters with the typewriter
a heavy black Victorian relic

that had been purchased by her Great Uncle
Phineas Beaverpelt van Otter
In one of his "modernizing" moments.

"The calling card has gone the way of snuff,"
He announced to the gathered relations,
"On this we shall type sentiments crisply."

He initiated a typing course
That quickly became known as "the broken nail,"
For ladies visiting the estate

The typewriter was mothballed, however,
when Phineas bought a horseless carriage
And began to tinker relentlessly.

Quarantine observed, "As Phineas was
A great modernizer, I have chosen
To become a divine pasturizer

A celebratrix of mechanical
Manifestations and complexities
And so on the "nail breaker I compose."

She had discovered the "Phineas Hulk,"
In a room filled with job boxes and shelves
That remained behind locked door for decades.

It had been a passion to discover
"Rooms behind key" in the sprawling mansion
Since she had first arrived as a small child

And at seventy, her entry into
This tiny container of curios
Off the main salon, and final unknown

Territory of her gigantic house
Produced simultaneous feelings of
Relief, fear, exhaustion and will to type.

She summoned the property mechanic
Larabee Smack and said, "What da ya think?"
Smack smacked a few keys, snorted and retired.

Quarantine arranged swift transportation
To the ancient Dutchess Lubratorium
Where the machine was oiled and restored

To full working order, "a great delight,"
She said, sitting before the hungry beast,
Rolling in a crisp high cotton paper

Striking the letter q, then fainting from
"the terrible exertion of the thing."
She did delight though in "assembling

Typists of the most remarkable
Character, talent, style, ability"
Who traveled by private coach to the manse

Stayed at her house, sometimes for many months
And, hootch fortified, confronted the hulk
With a mix of trepidation and vim.

Incomplete Sentences

Libby Medina, also known as
The plus prefect, was master of the
Incomplete sentence, "I don't like…"
She'd say, as closure was not her forte.

She had a small, smartly furnished,
Studio by the Gare Du Monde, called the
Filling Station, where she prepared unique
Edible sheets of *lines undone*, for the

Chicly dressed *Intellisensia*, fetishists of
The partial thought set down on paper,
Who would sip Pernod, and battle over
"How best to end this exquisite torture."

Joining in a cry of, "Eat The Sheets,"
When the last sentence on the page had been
Wrestled to a suitable conclusion
Then tearing it to bits, and enjoying

The ritual of smearing the pieces
With harissa, wadding them in tight balls
Popping them in their mouths, to be washed down
With *Illuminati,* a Belgian Ale.

And so it went for a time, until the…
Essay/. I am referring of course to
Manicotti Rabinowitz's
Critique cum character sketch, "The

Hipness of Elipsis…" following on
The less than stellar reception of her
"Novel of the suburban aesthetic,"
"Middlebrow: A Study of Tract House Taste."

Manicotti's comeback critical bomb
Detailing the social construction
Of the incomplete as *petit four*
Brought inevitable consequences

As Medina's methods became fodder
For popular culture. First came couture.
The Montreal Designer, Saint Lawrence
Seaway, revealed his trailblazing line of

"Dot Dresses," at his Fall season runway
show in Paris, and In Spring, Mum Des Garcons
A Naughty British Milf whose swimwear line
Had become garb de rigueur on mega-yachts

Tooling about the Mediterranean,
And the Grenadines during high season
Released her triple dot bathing suit
Spawning the pop-up, "Triple Dot Cocktail Bar"

First seen at Cannes during the Film Festival,
Then by Bryant Park at New York 's Fashion Week
And then In a Binghamton mini-Mall.
"The Triple Dot Cocktail Bar's" method

Of removing one or more ingredients
From standard cocktail recipes by
Throw of the dice spread virally through the
World of shakers, garnishes and muddles

Slews of unemployed creative writing
Graduates typing unfinished lines
On vintage blue Olivettis in the
Back of bar kitchens for illiterates.

Soon the Pernod sipping"incompletists"
Were gone, the Filling Station was empty
And Libby had departed, "perhaps,"
Said some, "on pilgrimage," but no one knew.

Of the original edible sheets
Only one example is known to remain,
Discovered tattered and scuffed by footprints
By the Filling Station's leasing agent.

Here (incompletely) it is reproduced:

For Your Dégustation

~ At the first moment...

~ ... and then her eyelashes...

~ Phillippe takes... pride in...

~ His circumspection...

~ As I wander in the Musée d'Orsay...

~ ... and through my cotton print dress on the first day of Spring...

~ His... and my ... on a barstool ...

~ And then again, she... at back table at Le Caveau de la Huchette

~ I sometimes wonder... and then...

~ The political is predictable; the sexual is not, but when the sexual becomes political, the state goes to...

~ A life of... is a life unspooled

~ today's small plates, will include... et sauce aux cèpes

~ seven lovers twirl about, of one...

~ ... but would you embrace the typists in Montmartre, whose dirty-fingered claques...

~ there I have been, and where...

~ I take solace in ... and pleasure by ...

~ and also... I did not say, but unwrapped your velvet gown...

~ ...when we are alone... also there is less said

~ ... but ...and... oh?...Oh?... oh! oh...oh...

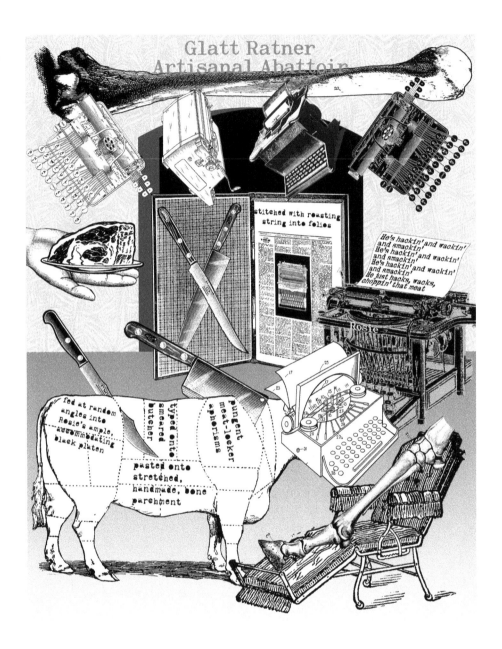

Glatt Ratner
Artisanal Abattoir

stitched with roasting
string into folios

He's hackin' and wackin'
and smackin'
He's hackin' and wackin'
and smackin'
He's hackin' and wackin'
and smackin'
He just hacks, wacks,
choppin' that meat

Rosie

fed at random
angles into
Rosie's ample,
accommodating
black platen

smeared
butcher

typed onto

pungent
meat-locker
aphorisms

pasted onto
stretched,
handmade, bone
parchment

The Bone Fragments

Glatt Ratner, butcher: a philosopher
of meat, known for the super-lean brisket
and a pot roast not only to die for
but to violate the 9th commandment
had a tiny office behind his shop

outfitted with a glass-keyed black beauty
named "Rosie," after his brown-bread best girl
who'd fallen under the Edgeware outbound
while waiting to return to Golders Green
after visiting friends in Camden Town.

Though it had been decades, he missed Rosie
Pining for her Zaftig figure daily
Writing her flowery letters every night
On periwinkle Selfridges' paper
Before turning to his Underground verse

Released periodically in calfskin
Bound chapbooks, series name, *Down to the Bone*
that distilled the lessons of a life spent
"Hackin', Whackin' and Smackin'," a la Roy Brown
in pungent meat-locker aphorisms

typed onto smeared butcher paper
fed at random angles into Rosie's
ample, accommodating black platen
pasted onto stretched, handmade, bone parchment
stitched with roasting string into folios

and delivered along with the brisket
to loyal readers who complained of chapped lips
a tip of the hat, a wink and a nod
slipping chapbooks under gabardine coats
to be read in bohemian cafes

then passed surreptitiously down the chain
of avid readers across London
who waited breath baited for the next bite,
the copies becoming frayed, tattered, torn
until mere bits, the storied, "Bone Fragments."

The Hunt and Pecks

Quinn Edward Dwight Hunt, known as Eskimo
and Reginald Townes Peck owned a dive bar,
the One Key, that had once been the One Note
a minimalist music establishment
that celebrated spare repetition
and musicians with the first name Johnny.

The One Key, festooned with dimly lighted
Typewriters arrayed on cocktail tables
Catered to stylish typing amateurs
Who'd come in to type each other mash notes
While throwing back the house special cocktail
The "Hunt and Peck," a confabulation

Of various liquors poured together
Vigorously shaken, then strained, contents
Changing at the whim of the forgetful
Barkeep, Eustace Fitzsimmons Sazarac Elmont
A mixologist of intuition
Grace and charm who always knew what to make

And how to deliver it with *Panache*,
A salty, savory Hunt and Peck snack
That kept patrons lustily drinking till dawn.
It was in one of these late night sessions
That a dilettante typist social club
The Hunt and Pecks came into existence.

They commissioned J. Press to make a tie
And a private jeweler to craft a ring
Whose crest was inscribed with HFWT
And whose inner band read H&Ps
And bore the motto, "Give me a finger."
First line of the customary greeting

That H&Ps would give to each other
At the strike of mutual recognition.
"Give me a finger."
"I'll type you the world."

Doings at the Cheesy Cover

Malaprop Titles reigned over the Cheesy.
Queen of the backroom burlesque typewriter
Extravanza and Hi-Tone revue
She had begun her career in dismay.
An unemployed reference librarian
And occasional burlesque performer
Known then by the handle, Miss Trixie Between
A camp follower of the Underground
And author of several "No-Doz" novels
Written in rabid caffeinated fits
Between episodes of masturbating
To a frayed photo of Charles Bukowski
She produced several classics of the form
But never developed a following.

There seemed to be a problem, a problem
With the titles. They seemed to come out wrong.
Her magisterial gin-soaked journey
Into the world of the old-money crowd
Portrayed through the eyes of an arriviste
Read as the perfect gender-bent fusion
Of the styles of Scott and Zelda F
As filtered through rhinestone-cornered cat glasses
Could have been the great American novel
But for the title, Backdoor to Paradise.
Her tense, manual typewriter, caper
Thrill ride, set hellishly in Desert Springs,
The Hand Job, was perhaps too indirect
For newsstand readers to guess its contents,
And her wistful melodramatic tale
Of an affair between two commuters
Who met when one got on a later train
Following an unfortunate incident
With a poorly stirred vodka martini
Pursued at a quaint neon motel

Located just between their villages
Once every four weeks for several decades
Might have tenderly awakened the hearts
Of her readers, had it not been titled,
A Time of the Month, we can speculate
But cannot know. What can be said is this:

Spotting Trixie crying in her coffee
At a shop catty-corner to the Cheesy
Zofred Mandelay Periwinkle Jones
Entered and attempted to console her
In a conversation that became legend.
"Your fictions are not your art," said Zofred
Owner and promoter of the Cheesy,
They are the method by which you arrive
At your true greatness, your genius expressed."
"Those are long words and quite vague," said Trixie
Dropping tears on an almond biscotto,
What on earth are you trying to tell me?"

"That it is not your stories, but the titles
In which your fanciful greatness resides.
Anyone can write a fictional book
Even people in the internet world
Who gather by the tens of thousands
During the same thirty-day month each year
To sit before the screen and bang out books
That no one will read, especially not
Their neglected spouses, friends and lovers.
After Umberto the novel's just Eco.
Pardon my pun, it's a nasty habit,
But the point is, your titles are alive,
So wipe your eyes with my fine silk hankie
Come across the street and begin to direct
Your first spectacular at the Cheesy."
"That's very kind...thoughtful" sniffled Trixie,
"but I'm not entirely following.

What's so great about my awful titles?"
"You poor dear child," said Zofred gently,
Your mislaid words are malaproptastic!
They unwittingly say two things at once
And that my dear is the soul of burlesque."
He dipped his finger in a water glass
Touched it to her forehead and said, "Trixie
Is no more. You are baptized and reborn
As the magnetic Malaprop Titles
And from this moment hence, your names shall grace
The madcap entertainments and delights
For which you and The Cheesy will be known."
Malaprop put a banana in her hair,
Walked arm in arm across the street with Zofred
And so began a beautiful friendship.

ii

But what of the Cheesy where Malaprop reigned?
It was a connection box, a junction, a beacon
For traveling typists stepping off the road
An aboveground hole for the Underground
Where news and gossip dripped like melted cheese
From the ubiquitous enamel fondue pots
With long-steel forks and wooden handles
Dipping sausage, apple and bread into
A mix of Gruyere and Emmentaler
Laced with white wine and mountain spices
That came to the table with Underbergs
To aid the digestion of the typists.

Zofred had founded the Cheesy, "because
you can't get good Raclette in this town,"
he is said to have said, but others think not.
Zofred was an avid collector of pulp,
A pursuit begun in his distant youth
Pursued passionately into adult life,
Driven by his love of cheesy covers,
Bearing such titles as, *The Tatooed Rood,*
Carnival of Lust, and *Midnight Sinners,*
But it was the taglines that steamed his blood,
"the brutal gamut of delinquency,"
"a strange story of twilight love...and hatred,"
"shore leave passions, their only escape..." and
"Whit Calderson thought he had tasted real passion..."
and it was these covers that gave the Cheesy life.
They were shellacked to the walls of the restrooms,
Frozen in epoxy in the two tops,
Framed like celebrity mugshots on the walls,
Embedded in the seats of the spinning barstools,
And printed on the backs of typists tabs,
Which would pile high on personal spikes
Until a manuscript fetched a price
Or a slumming swell looking for hot type
And some tweedy action picked up the bill.

Samizdat

The Samizdat Tea House
A steamed window storefront
With faded aqua walls
And silver samovars
On a long thin sideboard
Covered in white linen
Known by the insiders
As Laredo, held text

Mountains of self-published
Revolutionary
Applied Social Theory
Typed with sip and biscuit
At the moaning tables
That cried under the weight
Of the heavy elbowed
Musty-coated Wobblies

Impassioned and grizzled
Their ancient gnarled hands
Depressing keys in trance
Of the Twenties, as if
By their labors, the clock
Ran before the Red Queen
Moving quickly nowhere
Dorian Greys reversed

Holding time reverie
As cartilage turned to bone
Under wrinkied knuckles
The size of castanets
Cracking with each keystrike,
Stored in wooden cubbies
In the workshop behind
The public room.

To enter one winked
At N. Glazkov Smithers
Who attended the door
With the weary vigor
Befitting his late years
And indomitable
Conviction that Labor
Would prevail through red type.

CODA

Hyacinth Coyote

Reborn on the hour, each hour,
a ritual of Spring Equinox
performed in a shuttered mountain lodge—
shake-shingled, hunch-shouldered, topping Thoreau's
"...undulating country of clouds,"
embraced in Melville's gaze from Arrowhead
dark bitten, bewitched, un-forgiven
haunted by un-pardoning Old Coot,

a premonition of Hawthorne's, perhaps,
or then again, simply nature's shakes
of trees on immovable granite.
Catching Monadnock winds blown eighty-miles
to the dense-massed-pile above Greylock Glen,
yawps and howls this purple-eyed trickster

delivers into the migrant sky.
Gape-mouthed, back-throated, shifting shapes of clouds,
rendering them as spirit animals
with each bawling burst, this scrawny scree-loper
announces the forgiveness of all sins,
dying and renewing at the clock chime
in twenty-four convulsive cycles:
This western born Hyacinth Coyote

sits—between kaotic convulsions—
at the dining table of the old lodge,
her pale blue Olivetti MP1
resting steady on the new-lacquered wood,
the dim glow of a tortoise-shell desk lamp
lighting its keys in the final hour

of the poised day that divides sun from moon.

text: (c) Marc Zegans / TwU images: (c) Eric Edelman. All rights reserved. [TwU]

CPSIA information can be obtained
at www.ICGtesting.com
Printed in the USA
FSHW010649291218